Contents

A human's tongue 2
A frog's tongue 4
A dog's tongue 6
A butterfly's tongue 8
An anteater's tongue 10
A hummingbird's tongue 12
A snake's tongue 14
A giraffe's tongue 16
A snail's tongue 18
A snapping turtle's tongue 20
Whose tongue is this? 22
Index 24

This is a tongue.

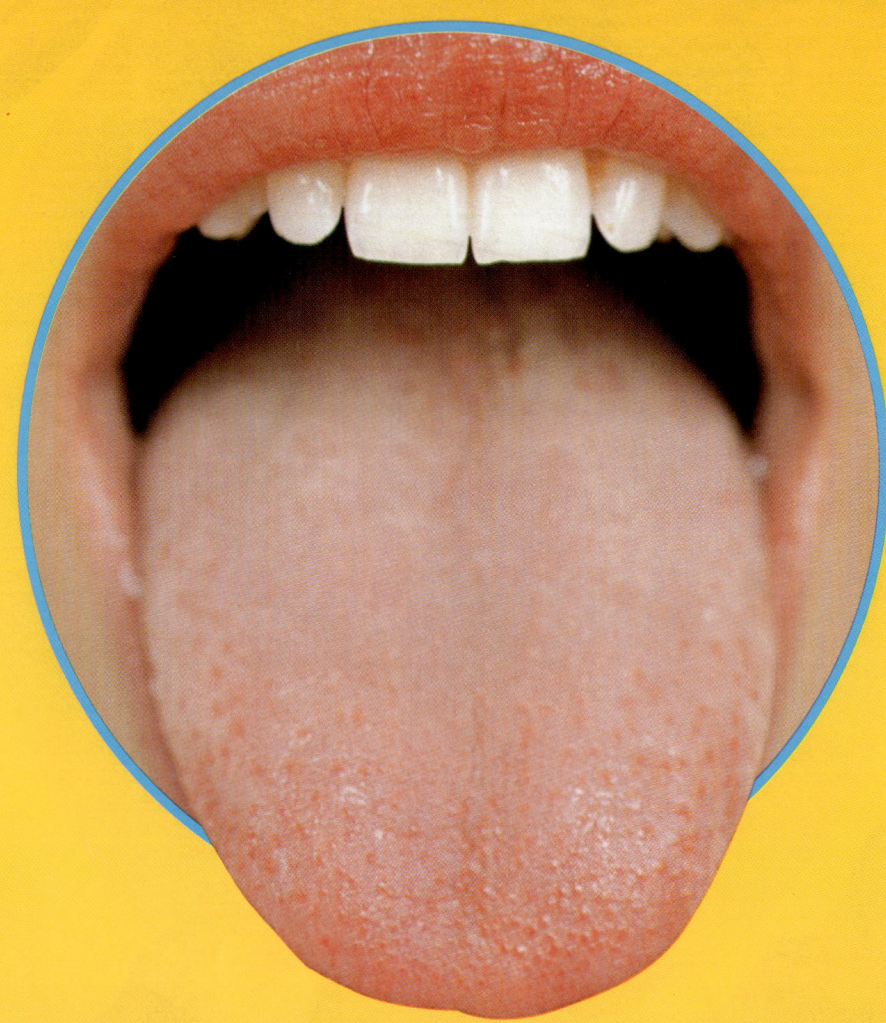

It is used to taste food.

This part of the tongue tastes **sour** food.

This part of the tongue tastes **bitter** food.

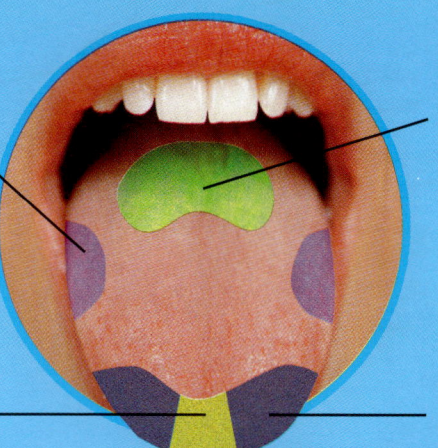

This part of the tongue tastes **sweet** food.

This part of the tongue tastes **salty** food.

This is a flicky, sticky tongue.

It shoots out to catch insects.

frog

This is a floppy, sloppy tongue.

It hangs in the air and helps keep the animal cool.

dog

This tongue is curled up.

tongue

It is used to sip the nectar from flowers.

tongue

butterfly

This tongue is very long and sticky.

It slips down small holes and licks up ants.

anteater

This tongue is like a tiny straw.

tongue

This tongue is forked.

It tastes the air to sense where food is.

snake

This tongue is like a hand.

tongue

It grabs the leaves on trees and pulls them off.

giraffe

This tongue is very, very rough.

tongue

This tongue plays a clever trick.

Small fish swim into the mouth to look at the tongue. Then they are trapped and eaten.

snapping turtle

Whose tongue is this?

Can you match the tongues on this page with the animals on page 23?

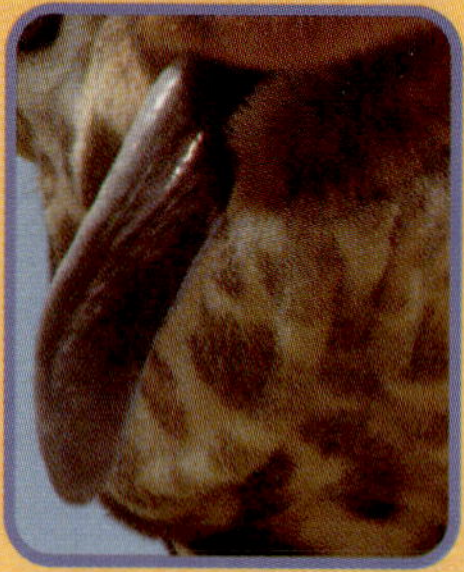

Index

air **7**, **15**
ants **11**

fish **21**
flowers **9**, **13**
food **3**, **15**, **19**

insects **5**

leaves **17**

nectar **9**

24